It's Not Easy Being God:
The Real George Soros

By Joy Tiz, MS, JD

Hero's Prose, LLC

It's Not Easy Being God: The Real George Soros

Copyright © 2010 Hero's Prose, LLC
Palm Desert, California 92260

First Printing: October 2010

ISBN-13: 978-0-61541-473-7
ISBN-10: 0-61541-473-7

Printed in the United States of America

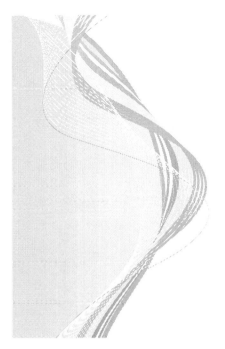

Table of Contents

Introduction

Georg eorge Soros was born in 1930 as Dzchdzhe Shorash, which was eventually anglicized to George Soros. The son of doting parents, Tivadar and Elizabeth, Soros developed his messianic delusion early in life, but had enough contact with reality to try to keep them mostly to himself. He's prone to the occasional lapse, however, as when a journalist joked he should be appointed Pope. Soros humbly responded: "I'm the Pope's boss now."

Tividar was an attorney who spent three years as a prisoner of war during World War I, followed by turbulent years spent in Russia from 1917 to 1920 — the early days of the revolution. He ultimately took refuge in the inhospitable Siberia.

George's dad impressed upon his son the importance of survival. He also inspired young George with his belief that during a revolution *anything* is possible — making revolution sound downright irresistible to a young boy.

The elder Soros had a knack for manipulating his way out of bad situations, which kept him from being seriously harmed during his captivity. As would be the case with George, Tividar had no guiding principles. "What side of the revolution was he on? Oh, both sides, of course." [1]

This is exactly the same approach George Soros takes when he injects himself into the politics of an unstable country. He can be, alternately a communist or a devout capitalist, as the occasion demands.

Soros sycophants would have us believe that Soros' collaboration with the Nazis was not of his own free choice, pointing out that he was a mere "child" at the time. True, he was a young lad of 14 — the age of reason in most jurisdictions.

Soros has had ample opportunity to redeem himself and denounce the atrocities committed by the Nazis against innocent Jews. Instead, when presented with a forum on the *60 Minutes* show, Soros displayed the cavernous lack of empathy associated with narcissism. "It created no problem at all," was Soros' response when questioned about his participation in the slaughter of Jews. [2]

Nor has his anti-Semitism abated with age.

> Self-hating Jew Soros openly says that he is not supportive of Israel. His reference to his Jewishness and perhaps to the fact that he does not donate to Jewish organizations: "It did not express itself in a sense of tribal loyalty that would have led [Soros] to support Israel." Somebody should interrupt him from counting his money long enough to explain to him that Israel is a nation not a 'tribe.' [3]

The Soros tentacles reach far and wide thanks to his great wealth and ability to keep himself behind the curtain. It would take an especially gifted forensic accountant to sort out all of the various interconnections among the major foundations and their smaller satellites, such as Annenberg or the Woods Fund. Barack Obama's mother, Ann Dunham, worked for the Ford Foundation in Indonesia along with the father of Treasury Secretary and tax cheat, Timothy Geithner. Even a cursory analysis of the relationship to the major charitable foundations to the career of Obama proves it is indeed a very small world after all.

The Soros-backed socialism and push toward a one-world government are the antithesis of Americanism. The Left has created mythologies about America and social justice that are in direct contradiction to historical facts. Rather than acknowledge the truth, the liberal resorts to distorting and misrepresenting the facts to support the false narrative.

Media Matters is deploying its considerable resources aiming at the Tea Party movement. The organization functions as a self-deputized fact checker primarily monitoring conservative commentators. They're not above doing some creative editing when deemed necessary. Big Bureaucracy:

> It's hardly surprising that Soros funds Media Matters, albeit somewhat indirectly. The OSI dumps millions on MoveOn, the Center for American Progress (CAP) and the Democracy Alliance. These organizations then donate to Media Matters. [4]

George Soros, via Media Matters is taking on the Tea Partiers:

> You know you've hit the big-time when George Soros takes notice. And you know you're making a tremendous difference when someone so well known goes to so much trouble to attempt to intimidate and bully you into silence. That's exactly what happened with the Cincinnati Tea Party's Tax Day Rally. George Soros-funded Media Matters decided to accuse the Cincinnati Tea Party of profiting because of charging more money for better seating for the event, part of which included a better view of the taping of the Sean Hannity show. [5]

Radical revisionism accelerated in the 1960s protest era. The decaying hippies of that era are responsible both for dumbing down your kids and preaching entirely false historical doctrine in which the United States is cast as the center of all that is evil and unjust in the world.

Never known for originality, the Sorosian Left ran in 2008 on the quotidian divide and conquer program. Liberals assign humans to groups that they then anoint with special victim status for the purpose of being used in their destructive power schemes. Liberals are obsessed with race. It harkens back to the old Soviet Union days in which blacks were openly recruited as operatives by the Kremlin to be exploited in the cause of destabilizing American democracy. Leftist policies will never be accepted by free people if the people know what they are. Liberals can only get their agenda through if they induce discord and chaos among the populace.

Race and class warfare are liberal contrivances. As Obama and the Pelosi/Reid cabal attempt to ram socialism down the collective American throat, note the anti- success, anti- capitalist bombast. Obama would have you believe that successful people can only achieve success by plundering the less prosperous. This is the grand deception upon which all forms of collectivism balance.

NOTES:

1. Slater, Robert. Soros, *The Life, Times & Trading Secrets of the World's Greatest Investor.* New York: McGraw-Hill, 1997.

2. 60 Minutes Interview. Kroft, Steve. 1998.

3. Mason, Jackie and Felder, Raoul. "The Sorry Tale of George Soros." *Jewish World Review.* Dec. 2, 2003. Retrieved from **http://www.jewishworldreview.com/1203/mason_soros. php3**

4. Valinska, Ellie. "Obama's Open Government, Soros's Open Society and Popper's Crazy Ideas." *Big Bureaucracy.* Feb. 2, 2010. **http://www.bigbureaucracy.com/?p=306**

5. Delaney, Elizabeth. *Examiner.com.* April 16, 2010. **http://www.examiner.com/christianity-politics-in-national/ soros-attempts-to-crash-cincinnati-tea-party-tax-day- rally-video**

~ 1 ~

It's Not Easy Being God

> I carried some rather potent messianic fantasies with me from childhood, which I felt I had to control otherwise they might get me into trouble.
>
> — George Soros

Obama's boss, George Soros discovered his own narcissism at an early age. Robert Slater, in his unauthorized biography of Soros– *Soros, The Life, Times & Trading Secrets of the World's Greatest Investor:*

> "Yet, what is one to make of a child who believed he was God?" [1]

Slater posits that such grandiose thoughts in childhood, if they were the "fleeting dreams of a small child" might be understandable if Soros had given any indication as an adult that he had outgrown his delusions.

> Yet, as an adult, he offered no sign, no dismissive gesture, no footnote signifying that he no longer clung to such wild convictions, but only the suggestion of how difficult it was for someone to believe himself a deity.[2]

In other words, Soros figured out early on that his messiah complex wasn't going to be well received in the real world and he should try to tone it down a bit.

He's having mixed results with that.

There are those who still cling doggedly to the fabrication that Soros is some kind of "philanthropist," despite overwhelming evidence to the contrary. The compassionate philanthropist has been pushing for human euthanasia for years.

The august altruist has long believed we made much too big of a fuss about 9/11, an event which he found inspiring: "Hijacking fully fueled airliners and using them as suicide bombs was an audacious idea, and its execution could not have been more spectacular."[3]

Poor George, like his Jackal in Chief, has carried the burden of being a god throughout his life:

A passage in his book *The Alchemy of Finance*, published in 1987, distinguishes Soros from all other financiers, ever. "I have always harbored an exaggerated view of my self-importance," he wrote.

> To put it bluntly, I fancied myself as some kind of god or an economic reformer like Keynes, or, even better, like Einstein. My sense of reality was strong enough to make me realise that these expectations were excessive, and I kept them hidden as a guilty secret. This was a source of considerable unhappiness through much of my adult life. As I made my way in the world, reality came close enough to my fantasy to allow me to admit my secret, at least to myself. Needless to say, I feel much happier as a result. [4]

In 2003, Soros figured out that he could force his repugnant ideas on America most efficiently by simply changing the government.

"'I've come to the conclusion,' Soros told Fortune, 'that one can do a lot more about the issues I care about by changing the government than by pushing the issues.'" In short, he has become the world's angriest billionaire."[5]

In 2006 and 2008, Soros made substantial progress toward his goal of changing the United States Government.

Though Soros and his Shadow Party failed to bring about 'regime change' in 2004, the vast network of interrelated Shadow Party groups would prove to be key players in the 2006 midterm elections that saw Democrats seize control of Congress. Of particular significance was Democracy Alliance, a non-tax-exempt nonprofit entity registered in the District of Columbia, which Soros had founded in 2005, and whose long-term objective was to develop a funding clearinghouse for leftist groups.

In 2008, Soros' Shadow Party was again a major force in the movement that not only expanded the Democratic Party's congressional majorities, but also delivered the presidency to Barack Obama.[6]

George Soros has orchestrated plenty of regime changes. Don't be fooled by the mythology that Soros was instrumental in opposing communism in Eastern Europe. Soros places himself on whichever side is most likely to net him the greatest power.

According to Slater, Soros is fascinated by chaos. "That's how I make my money: understanding the revolutionary process in financial markets."[7]

If it's chaos Soros is looking for, he's got the right cipher in the White House.

NOTES:

1. Slater, Robert. *Soros: The Life, Times & Trading Secrets of the World's Greatest Investor*. New York: McGraw-Hill, 2009.

2. Ibid, Pg. 15

3. Soros, George. "The Bubble Of American Supremacy." *The Atlantic Monthly*, December 2003.

4. Soros, George. *Alchemy of Finance*, 1987.

5. Gimein, Mark. "George Soros Is Mad As Hell. *Fortune* Oct. 27, 2003.

6. *DiscovertheNetworks.org*. George Soros. **http://www.discoverthenetworks.org/individualProfile. asp?indid=977**

7. Slater, pg. 47

- 2 -

Who's Afraid of the Big Bad Soros?

Democrats have a Nazi collaborator, literally—international financier George Soros—funding their phony grassroots organizations.

— Ann Coulter

In a 1998 interview with Steve Kroft, George Soros acknowledged forging documents and pretending to be Christian to save himself from the Nazis, for which he feels no guilt or sorrow. "I was fourteen," Soros said. "My character was made then."[1] Regarding his participation in confiscating valuables from innocent Jews, and serving death camp warrants, Soros told Kroft, "It created no problem at all."[2] Soros has no sense that he shouldn't be there; he felt he was a mere spectator. Soros rationalizes his behavior: "If I didn't do it, someone else would."[3]

Thus, it makes perfect sense that Soros is the de facto head of the Democratic Party in America now that it is a foaming-at-the-mouth, rabid, left-wing Democratic Party. As David Horowitz and Richard Poe put it, "Soros and his Shadow Party did not invent the politics of demagoguery and racial division. They are merely practicing and expanding the politics familiar on the Democratic Left."[4] There is seldom any originality on the left.

In 1979, Soros set up his misnamed foundation, the Open Society Institute (OSI). The OSI is the hub of the Shadow Party's operation, doling out tens of millions of dollars every year to radical organizations to further the Soros agenda:

- Promoting the view that America is institutionally an oppressive nation.

- Promoting the election of leftist political candidates throughout the United States.

- Opposing virtually all post-9/11 national security measures enacted by U.S. government, particularly the Patriot Act.

- Depicting American military actions as unjust, unwarranted and immoral.

- Promoting open borders, mass immigration, and a watering down of current immigration laws.

- Promoting a dramatic expansion of social welfare programs funded by ever-escalating taxes.

- Promoting social welfare benefits and amnesty for illegal aliens.

- Defending the civil rights and liberties of suspected anti-American terrorists and their abettors.

- Financing the recruitment and training of future activist leaders of the political Left.

- Advocating America's unilateral disarmament and/or a steep reduction in its military spending.

- Opposing the death penalty in all circumstances.

- Promoting socialized medicine in the United States.

- Promoting the tenets of radical environmentalism, whose ultimate goal, as writer Michael Berliner has explained, is 'not clean air and clean water, [but] rather ... the demolition of technological/industrial civilization.'

- Bringing American foreign policy under the control of the United Nations.

- Promoting racial and ethnic preferences in academia and the business world alike.

- Promoting taxpayer-funded abortion-on-demand.

- Advocating stricter gun-control measures.

- Advocating the legalization of marijuana.[5]

Richard Poe explains how Soros was able to dragoon the entire Democratic party:

> The Shadow Party is the real power driving the Democrat machine. It is a network of radicals dedicated to transforming our constitutional republic into a socialist hive.
>
> The leader of these radicals is ... George Soros. He has essentially privatized the Democratic Party, bringing it under his personal control. The Shadow Party is the instrument through which he exerts that control....
>
> It works by siphoning off hundreds of millions of dollars in campaign contributions that would have gone to the Democratic Party in normal times, and putting those contributions at the personal disposal of Mr. Soros. He then uses that money to buy influence and loyalty where he sees fit.
>
> In 2003, Soros set up a network of privately-owned groups which acts as a shadow or mirror image of the Party. It performs all the functions we would normally expect the real Democratic Party to perform, such as shaping the Party platform, fielding candidates, running campaigns, and

so forth. However, it performs these functions under the private supervision of Mr. Soros and his associates.

The Shadow Party derives its power from its ability to raise huge sums of money. By controlling the Democrat purse strings, the Shadow Party can make or break any Democratic candidate by deciding whether or not to fund him.

During the 2004 election cycle, the Shadow Party raised more than $300 million for Democrat candidates, prompting one of its operatives, MoveOn PAC director Eli Pariser, to declare, 'Now it's our party. We bought it, we own it....'[6]

In his book, *The Age of Fallibility*, Soros writes, 'The main obstacle to a stable and just world order is the United States.'[7] He announced in 2003 that it is necessary to 'puncture the bubble of American supremacy.'[8] Soros is working systematically to achieve that goal.

Keeping in mind that Soros will always act in ways that provide maximum benefit to Soros, what are his plans for Obama? It's clear he found the cult leader he needed. Obama is performing correctly with his daily catastrophizing and power grabbing. Obama is giving Soros four to eight years to work in the shadows to destroy America and grab what spoils he can. Nobody knows more about how to destroy a currency than Soros. We have to question whether the peculiar short-selling patterns in the fall of 2008 and the over-hyped economic "collapse" were staged to get Obama elected.

It's astonishing that so many commentators seem genuinely confused about the real power behind the Democrats. They talk about Obama's plans as if he were some kind of normal president who just happens to be very bad at it. In reality, Obama has little sway over his own operation. All the ruminating about whether Obama will now move toward the center or modify his policies to reflect the will of the people is sophomoric. It is naive to suggest that Obama has the freedom to run afoul of his boss's orders.

Soros also is working to throw out our Constitution and replace it with his own version. In the *American Thinker*:

> In April 2005, Soros' Open Society Institute was the primary sponsor of a conference at Yale Law School, called, 'The Constitution in 2020.' The conference's task was to produce 'a progressive vision of what the Constitution ought to be.'
>
> When one sees references in progressive speak about the 'evolutionary character of constitutional law,' they are talking about changing the Constitution to formally enshrine their policy preferences so they can avoid the messy necessity of having to win elections. (Shadow Party; Horowitz and Poe; p. 71)"[8]

As the left forces nationalized health care on us, we may want to consider the George Soros-funded Project on Death in America. Soros is a leading promoter of the assisted suicide movement. He papers over it with tripe about compassion. In reality, the project is a push for palliative care rather than treatment for gravely ill patients.

The Democrat economic platform is entirely Soros-friendly.

'"There is a general concern with sovereign debt,' Soros said. 'It is coming under suspicion and it has a political momentum, because there is increasing political resistance to allowing national debt to rise.'"[9] Soros griped at Davos about America's biliousness over running up massive deficits. Obama's catastrophic budget was hauled in via heavy equipment shortly after Soros's pro-debt directive.

Soros got his guy into the White House. Next on his agenda: the Velvet Revolution. This is a term used in Eastern Europe to describe the sort of bloodless coup for which Soros is known in that part of the world. He has used these methods to topple regimes in many countries, including Yugoslavia, Ukraine and the Republic of Georgia.

Soros' velvet revolutions requires waiting for an election, then generate a crisis by charging voter fraud.

How interesting that just the other day, Barack Obama made a peculiar statement during his daily whine fest about being accused of behaving like a Bolshevik.

Too few commentators are informing the people about the dangers of Soros. Ann Coulter is one of the few willing to speak the truth about this pariah. Glenn Beck has tied Soros to the Democrats. The alternative media talk show hosts occasionally bandy the Soros name about, acknowledging that Soros is a bad egg, but failing to warn the American people about the character and ambition that is now driving the president and both houses of congress.

Thus, one of the most dangerous men in the world gets to stay below the radar. Few Americans know much about Soros. Many actually consider George Soros to be some sort of philanthropist. But Soros acts solely to improve the Soros condition. Despite the lofty-sounding rhetoric about an open society, Soros' objective is to wreck the United States.

> The Shadow Party operates through deception. It uses the Democratic Party as camouflage. By posing as ordinary Democrats, Shadow Party candidates trick mainstream voters into supporting them. Their true agenda remains concealed. As Soros writes in *The Age of Fallibility*, '[T]he Democratic Party does not stand for the policies that I advocate; indeed, if it did, it could not be elected.'" [10]

Only a small fraction of the media — often referred to as alternative — are willing to examine the actual facts about the mysterious man who became leader of the free world. Talk radio and independent bloggers have become the modern version of Nazi resistors with their chain letters and ham radios.

Why is it that without the blogosphere, there would be no discussion of George Soros and his full-scale war on the United States?

NOTES

1. *60 Minutes Interview*, Steve Kroft, 1998.

2. Ibid

3. Ibid

4. Horowitz, David and Poe, Richard, *The Shadow Party: How George Soros, Hillary Clinton and Sixties Radicals Seized Control of the Democratic Party.* 2006. Thomas Nelson.

5 *DiscovertheNetworks.org*. George Soros.
   http://www.discoverthenetworks.org/individualProfile.asp?indid=977

6. Horowitz, David and Poe, Richard, *The Shadow Party*.

7. Soros, George. *The Age of Fallibility*.

8. Shriver, Kyle-Anne, "George Soros and the Alchemy of Regime Change." *American Thinker*. Feb. 27, 2008.

9. Stewart, Heather. "Bank of England Policymakers Split Over Prospects for British Economy." The Guardian. 27, Jan. 2010.

10. Soros, *Age of Fallibility*. 2006. Public Affairs.

- 3 -

George Soros: International Man of Misery

The term "euphemism" refers to the substitution of a vague or milder term for one that may be considered harsh, offensive or blunt.

Example:
George Soros is a "philanthropist."

If by "philanthropist" we mean one who creates chaos, destruction and financial ruin for his own personal gain, it's a perfect fit. Calling Soros a philanthropist is rather like referring to the Nazi block wardens as Neighborhood Watch.

Soros certainly gives lots of money away. But a philanthropist acts to improve the human condition. Soros acts solely to improve the Soros condition. Despite the lofty sounding rhetoric about an Open Society, Soros' objective is to wreck the United

States. Actually Soros never really defines his Open Society. The concept arose in the 1930s with the notion of a moral code based on "universal principles." After tweaking the concept to suit his own purposes, Soros adopted his own version of an Open Society which would be one in which the U.S. has no power.

Soros was born in Hungary in 1930 to non-practicing Jewish parents. His father, a lawyer, was able to hide their identities, and young George was recruited by the Judenrat to hand out flyers deceptively directing Jews to turn themselves in for deportation to the death camps. Soros later said he found the work exhilarating. Later, passing himself as an official's godson, he accompanied his benefactor, confiscating valuables from innocent Jews.[1]

Soros would later tell Steve Kroft on *60 Minutes* that he had no remorse about what he had done.

In fact, Soros doesn't have remorse for much, if anything. In The Shadow Party, Soros is quoted as saying that conscience clouds an investor's judgment.[2]

Soros amassed his fortune by speculating in the currency markets. He got a lot of attention for tanking the British pound in 1992. More than once, Soros has used his status as an investor to manipulate markets. According to Horowitz and Poe, the great patriot Soros likely sold short after 9/11 when the rest of the nation was being urged to take whatever they could afford and buy some shares of their favorite stocks.[3] Lots of patriotic Americans did exactly that.

To further jeopardize our national security, Soros told CNN that the market would react negatively if the U.S. were to invade Afghanistan, knowing his words would cause a global market reaction. Soros has stuck his nose in governments all over the world claiming a philanthropic motive. Yet like night into day, once he's done, the local economy is in a shambles and Soros is richer.

According to journalist Anne Williamson, Soros appeared before the House Banking Committee in September, 1999, attempting to explain to stunned congressmen exactly how so many U.S. taxpayer dollars had evaporated in Russia. The Clintons managed to shut that scandal down quickly thanks to their expertise in scandal control.

Soros was actually convicted of insider trading in France. His opinion moves markets. He is one of the most powerful people in the world entirely due to his ability to get other people to part with their money. His tentacles are everywhere. He uses numerous foundations and associations to keep money flowing and spread around. It's no secret that George Soros is fond of deceit and subterfuge. For all of the nonsensical blathering he does about how he can make the world a better place, he has no real plan to do any such thing. Soros loses interest in a project after the demo phase is over. According to Horowitz and Poe, Soros candidly admits he finds destruction easier than creation.

Thus it makes perfect sense that Soros is the de facto head of the Democratic Party in America now that it is a foaming- at- the-mouth rabid left wing Democratic Party. As Horowitz and Poe put it: "Soros and his Shadow Party did not invent the politics of demagoguery and racial division. They are merely practicing and expanding the politics familiar on the Democratic Left."[4]

In 2004 Soros made it his personal mission to defeat George W. Bush. Not only did Bush not share his moral relativism and radical ideology, Soros was outraged about Afghanistan and Iraq. Soros opposed Bush's War on Terror and provides funding to pro terror groups. Worse still from Soros' point of view, after enjoying easy access to the Clintons, Bush was not equally impressed and failed to seek out his wise counsel on foreign policy.

John Kerry's loss in 2004 was gasoline on the fire. "This is the Sorosization of the Democratic Party," say Rachel Ehrenfelt and Shawn MacComber. "As we will see, this idea of 'scruples' being for the other guy has been central to Soros' philosophy in business, philanthropy and foreign policy." [5]

Although Soros had a mutually beneficial relationship with the Clintons, he knew enough to hedge his bets in 2008 and back more than one candidate. The type of revolution Soros wants requires a charismatic figure that can create a mass movement. Soros himself actually dislikes publicity. Good oratory skills and personal charisma are what he needs. Soros himself prefers to stay below the radar and work his subterfuge behind the scenes. After all, "Soros' main concern is that somebody be elected who is indebted enough to him to pick up the phone when he calls." [6]

Just the other day, I attended a speech by Peggy Noonan. The topic was presidents. She told funny stories and shared her insights into presidents Bush, Reagan, Clinton and Obama. Noonan talked about Clinton's personal charisma, saying, "it was impossible not to look at him." She said his speeches were well delivered but remarkably lacking in substance. Is anyone seeing a pattern here?

Noonan sees Obama as more like Clinton than anyone else, not only in his policies, but his presentation.

Is it possible then that Bill Clinton was supposed to fulfill the role of George Soros' cult-leading Messiah but simply failed at it?

Soros can't wreak his havoc alone. He needs his puppets.

It's important to understand that George Soros doesn't want to "change" America. He wants to destroy it. America in its current state is anathema to Soros. The current Oval Office occupant is not particularly fond of America either. His association with America-hating radicals should be enough for most people, but let's not overlook the fact that his very first sit-down interview after becoming president was to al Arabyia News Channel. Obama took the opportunity to share his views with the Muslim world that America has behaved very badly and we can be expected to change our ways so our relationship with Muslims will be like it was "20 or 30 years ago." This is a bit perplexing unless Obama either knows less about history than we thought or he longs for the days when Islamofascists, led by Khomeini were holding 52 American hostages. I daresay the Muslim world was cheered to learn that our new president plans to take us back to the happy halcyon days of the Carter Administration.

When Soros gets hold of power in any government, he makes money. It is difficult to find examples of Soros invasions that leave the target country better off. But that is not Soros' concern. Obama's monstrous Stimulus Bill (euphemisms again) fits neatly into Soros' paradigm. You can read Soros' economy recovery plan on the *Huffington Post*. (Feb. 12, 2009)

For all the posturing Soros does about creating his Marxist Utopia there is no actual plan to create a new social order, an open one or otherwise. Soros, for all of his rambling hasn't thought it through that far and he is not going to. His interest begins and ends with his potential to exploit whomever he can to grab money and power. He actually makes garden-variety dopey liberals rather endearing by comparison. At least some of them believe in their unrealistic vision of socialism.

Keeping in mind that Soros will always act in ways that provide maximum benefit to Soros, what are his plans for Obama? It's clear he found the puppet he needed. Obama is performing correctly with his daily catastrophizing and power grabbing. But what would benefit Soros more: a successful Obama presidency or a failed one? Success would give Soros four to eight years to work in the Shadows to destroy America and grab what spoils he can. But a failed presidency could offer even more. Obama and his Ministry of Propaganda have managed to create fear and panic in the population. His policies, if implemented, cannot but lead to economic trouble and eventual shortages and rationing. Nobody knows more about how to destroy a currency than Soros. If an inept, inexperienced and radical president has his way, which Obama surely will, the net result is pretty predictable. Is that kind of social and economic chaos designed to open up a power vacuum that a guy like Soros just can't resist?

NOTES

1. David Horowitz and Richard Poe. *The Shadow Party: How George Soros, Hillary Clinton and Sixties Radicals Seized Control of the Democratic Party.* 2006. Thomas Nelson.

2. Ibid.

3. Ibid

4. Ibid.

5. Ehrenfelt, Rachel and MacComber, Shawn. *Frontpagemagazine.com*, 28, Oct. 2004.

6. Ibid.

- 4 -

The Bear
We Could
Have Tamed

The Clinton administration allowed It's-Not-Easy-Being-God Soros to run wild in the dying Soviet Union. The results were entirely predictable. Working in tandem with Strobe Talbott, Russian Policy Czar, they set about playing games with government funds. Soros reveled in having so much access to the Clintons and fancied himself part of the "Clinton team." Clinton squandered the opportunity to help the Russian people form a healthy democracy and instead allowed Soros and his team to profiteer, leaving the country in shambles.[1]

Kyle-Anne Shriver in American Thinker:

> He [Soros] had already been widely proclaiming that it was his own machinations that brought

down the Soviet Empire. When asked about his sphere of influence in the Soviets' demise for a *New Republic* interview in 1994, Mr. Soros humbly replied that the author ought to report that 'the former Soviet Empire is now called the Soros Empire.'[2]

When our House Banking Committee investigated the Russia-gate scandal in 1999, trying to determine just how $100 billion had been diverted out of Russia, forcing the collapse of its currency and the default of its enormous loans from the International Monetary Fund, Soros was called to testify. He denied involvement of course, but finally admitted that he *had* used insider access in a deal that was barred to foreign investors to acquire a huge chunk of Sidanko Oil.

The Russia scandal was labeled by Rep. Jim Leach, then head of the House Banking Committee, to be 'one of the greatest social robberies in human history.'[3]

Of course, Russia-gate was quickly hushed up and pushed aside in the public's lurid, and quite insatiable, interest in Monica-gate.[4]

Last year, as the Polish people were solemnizing the 70th anniversary of the Soviet invasion, Barack Obama, brandishing the narcissist's characteristic heartlessness, announced he was reneging on America's promise to provide missile defense in Eastern Europe. [5]

As reported in *BloggerNews*:

> The timing of Obama's announcement upset Poland and Polish Americans because it came on Sept. 17, the 70th anniversary of the Russian invasion of Poland at the beginning of World War II. The U.S. Embassy in Warsaw also pointed out that 'Russian troops occupied Poland for the next five decades, and did not withdraw until after the Cold War.' It was not a classic military occupation by a foreign power, since the communist regime in Poland had its own army and police and Soviet troops were confined to military bases, but all major decisions regarding Poland's foreign and domestic policy had to have Moscow's approval—something the Poles fear might happen again if the United States disengages militarily from the region. [6]

Polish President Lech Kaczynski, his wife, Maria, and a large swath of the Polish government died in a plane crash bound for the Katyn memorial. Kaczynski, a stalwart anti-communist, was angry with Putin for his long refusal to accept Russia's guilt in the slaughter of Polish citizens by Stalin's secret police.

The Boston Globe:

> Certain dates, events, and places become
> emblems of unforgettable suffering for an entire
> people. Auschwitz holds that meaning for Jews,
> as does the 1915 death march for Armenians or
> the 1922 Smyrna massacre for Greeks. Polish
> memory is haunted by the Red Army's execution
> of 22,000 Polish officers and intellectuals in the
> Katyn forest in the spring of 1940. [7]

KGB Hit Man in Chief Vladimir Putin made a "belated gesture
of reconciliation" toward the people of Poland last Wednesday
when he laid a wreath at a Katyn gravesite. Belated indeed:

> During the communist era, Polish schoolchildren
> were taught that the Katyn crimes were committed
> by the Nazis. Poles knew this was an official
> lie. Finally, in 1992, then-Russian President Boris
> Yeltsin ended the lies by releasing a copy of a
> Stalin-era document resolving to kill the Polish
> prisoners because they were 'inveterate and
> incorrigible enemies of the Soviet power.'[8]

There is no dispute that the president's plane, a Russian-built Tupolev Tu-154 is a junk box.[9] The plane was overhauled last December, including service to both the engines — at Aviakor avia-
tion in Samara, Russia. [10]

The flight data recorders have been recovered in Russia. Thus, Putin will oversee the investigation, which is a lot like having Eric Holder investigate SEIU.

The people of Poland have suffered a decapitation of their government. The world has lost a strong voice for democracy and freedom. America has to face the ugly reality that our president is determined to abuse our allies and cosset our enemies. And one thing none of us can expect from Putin is the truth.

NOTES

1. Horowitz and Poe, *The Shadow Party: How George Soros, Hillary Clinton and Sixties Radicals Seized Control of the Democratic Party.* 2006

2. Shriver, Kyle-Anne, "George Soros and the Alchemy of 'Regime Change." *American Thinker,* Feb. 27, 2008. Retrieved from **http://www.americanthinker.com/2008/02/george_soros_and_the_alchemy_o.html**

3. Horowitz and Poe, *The Shadow Party* p. 96.

4. Ibid. *American Thinker.*

5. Tiz, Joy. "America's Crash Course in Narcissism 101." Jan. 25. 2010. Retrieved from **http://joytiz.com/2010/americas-crash-course-in-narcissim-101/**

6. Blogger News Network. Sept. 29, 2009. **http://www.bloggernews.net/122432**

7. "Putin: Easing the Burden of Memory." *Boston Globe* editorial. April 10, 2010. Retrieved from **http://www.boston.com/bostonglobe/editorial_opinion/editorials/articles/2010/04/10/putin_easing_the_burden_of_memory/**

8. Medetsky, Anatoly. Katyn Commemorations Mark "Turnaround." *The Moscow Times.* April 8, 2010. **http://www.themoscowtimes.com/news/article/katyn-commemorations-mark-turnaround/403542.html**

9. Cutler, David. "Factbox: Key facts about the Tupolev Tu-154 airliner." Reuters. April 10, 2010. **http://www.reuters.com/article/idUSTRE6391G820100410**

10. *Flight Global.* "Investigators begin analysing Polish Tu-154's recorders. "Nov. 4, 2010. **http://www.flightglobal.com/articles/2010/04/11/340490/investigators-begin-analysing-polish-tu-154s-recorders.html**

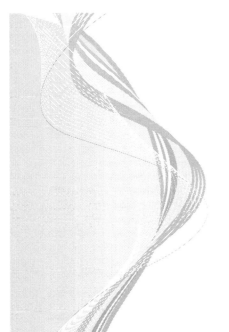

- 5 -

Soros: Don't Blame Me

Ed Lasky at American Thinker explains how Obama's Puppet Master, unrepentant Nazi collaborator, George Soros, enjoys the benefits of liberal hypocrisy as well as America's misery:

> The Democratic Party preaches that it is for the little guy and bashes Wall Street and bankers mercilessly. Yet it remains silent on the machinations of their patron saint, George Soros. He funds think tanks galore. He created the Center for American Progress—Obama's think-tank and hiring hall. The CAP is an adjunct of the Democratic Party, peddling its ideas throughout the media landscape. Soros has an empire of 527 groups he uses to elect

> Democrats and promote their policies. He is *the* top funder of such shadowy groups, and his billionaire political allies—Peter Lewis, Herb and Marion Sandler—also big funders of the CAP, round up the top five. Soros was an early and ardent supporter of Barack Obama—even using a loophole in federal campaign loans to exceed normal limits on donations.[1]

Soros maintains a super secret hedge fund, the Quantum Fund, which is held overseas. As Democrats posture about how they care for the little guy, they take great care to protect Soros and his hedge fund investors.

We keep hearing a lot of commotion about the need to regulate hedge funds, but very little has been done. There is no requirement that hedge funds domiciled overseas (as is Soros') disclose the identities of investors.

Lasky warned in February that the next caper would be an assault on the Euro:

> Some heavyweight hedge funds have launched large bearish bets against the euro in moves that are reminiscent of the trading action at the height of the U.S. financial crisis. The big bets are emerging amid gatherings such as an exclusive 'idea dinner 'earlier this month

> that included hedge-fund titans SAC Capital Advisors LP and Soros Fund Management LLC. During the dinner, hosted by a boutique investment bank at a private townhouse in Manhattan, a small group of all-star hedge-fund managers argued that the euro is likely to fall to 'parity'—or equal on an exchange basis—with the dollar, people close to the situation say.[2]

Betting on the fall of the Euro creates an opportunity to make enormous amounts of money.

The *Daily Mail* is straightforward:

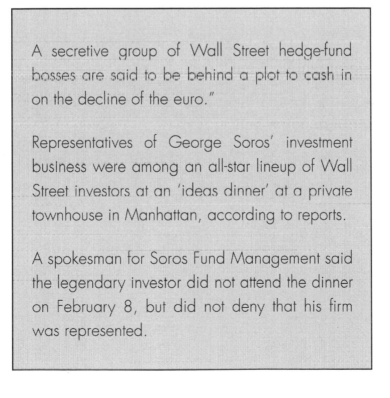

> A secretive group of Wall Street hedge-fund bosses are said to be behind a plot to cash in on the decline of the euro."
>
> Representatives of George Soros' investment business were among an all-star lineup of Wall Street investors at an 'ideas dinner' at a private townhouse in Manhattan, according to reports.
>
> A spokesman for Soros Fund Management said the legendary investor did not attend the dinner on February 8, but did not deny that his firm was represented.

At the dinner, the speculators are said to have argued that the euro is likely to plunge in value to parity with the dollar.

The single currency has been under enormous pressure because of Greece's debt crisis, plus financial worries in Portugal, Italy, Spain and Ireland.

But, it has also struggled because hedge funds have been placing huge bets on the currency's decline, which could make the speculators hundreds of millions of pounds.

The euro traded at $1.51 in December, but has since fallen to $1.34. Details of the secretive dinner emerged days after Mr. Soros, chairman of Soros Fund Management, warned in a newspaper article that the euro could 'fall apart' even if the European Union can agree a deal to shore up support for stricken Greece.

Mr. Soros, who made more than $1 billion by currency speculation when the pound was ejected from the Exchange Rate Mechanism on Black Wednesday in 1992, believes the structure of the euro is 'patently flawed.'[3]

Soros, in an interview with Bloomberg Radio: "It is a make or break time for the euro. It's a question whether the political will to hold Europe together is there or not." [4]

Soros has already castigated the Jackal in Chief of the United States for his failure to submerge the U.S. into deep enough debt. Now the Puppet Master is admonishing the EU for charging market interest rates on its bailout to Greece, which could have the unfortunate consequence of forcing spending cuts.[5]

Through his financial machinations, George Soros has amassed an astonishing amount of power, not just in the United States, but worldwide. A few well-placed words from Soros can move markets.

As the Puppet in Chief and the lame duck congress force the same economic policies on us that are bringing down the EU, the Puppet Master bewails his scapegoat status:

According to *BlackListedNews*:

> Claiming that Soros is not involved in any wrong-doing, Michael Vachon, a spokesman for Soros Fund Management, told the *Times*: 'It has become commonplace to direct attention toward George Soros whenever currency markets are in the news."[6]

It's not easy being God.

NOTES

1. Lasky, Ed. Soros, "Obama, and the Millionaires Exception." *American Thinker*. April 30, 2007.

2. Ibid.

3. West, Karl. "Man who broke the Bank of England, George Soros, at centre of hedge funds plot to cash in on fall of the euro"; *The Daily Mail*. Feb. 27, 2010. Retrieved from **http://www.dailymail.co.uk/news/worldnews/article-1253791/Is-man-broke-Bank-England-George-Soros-centre-hedge-funds-betting-crisis-hit-euro.html**

4. Bloomberg Business Week. "Soros Says EU Should Offer Greece Cheaper Loans." April 9, 2010 **http://www.businessweek.com/news/2010-04-09/soros-says-greece-needs-cheaper-loans-to-avoid-death-circle-.html**

5. Ibid.

6. *Blacklisted News*. "George Soros' Anti-Capitalist Agenda Plans to Loot Companies & Countries." March 7, 2010.

- 6 -

Soros Plots Plunder of 2012 Election

> *The people who cast the votes don't decide an election, the people who count the votes do.*
>
> — Joseph Stalin

A s the rest of us count the days until the November election, Obama's boss, unrepentant Nazi collaborator, George Soros, is brewing a scheme to pirate the 2012 presidential election. Still smarting from the trauma of losing to George W. Bush in 2004, Soros is concocting ever more perfidious schemes for ensuring the outcome of our next presidential election.

The phony philanthropist, who thinks he's God, is funding the SOS project, conniving to install regime-friendly operatives in secretaries of state offices nationwide. Matthew Vadum unveils the plot:

> The vehicle for this planned hijacking of democracy is a below-the-radar non-federal '527' [Thank you, John McCain] group called the Secretary of State Project. The entity can accept unlimited financial contributions and doesn't have to disclose them publicly until well after the election.[1]
>
> The founders of the Secretary of State Project, which claims to advance 'election protection' but only backs Democrats, religiously believe that right-leaning secretaries of state helped the GOP steal the presidential elections in Florida in 2000 (Katherine Harris) and in Ohio in 2004 (Ken Blackwell).

SoS was co-founded by James Rucker, former director for Moveon. org Civic Action. Moveon.org is of course, funded by Soros. Soros is one of the more notable contributors to the SoS project.[2]

SoS was instrumental in abetting freak show refugee Al Franken's senate seat depredation by way of Soros factotum, Minnesota Secretary of State Mark Ritchie:

> The SoS website lauds Ritchie as 'arguably the most progressive secretary of state in America,'

> and states: 'Thanks to SoS Project donors, Minnesota's Mark Ritchie—a true champion for Democracy—was able to defeat a two-term incumbent Republican by less than 5 points. We helped close the gap and make the difference with cable television ads targeting women and seniors.' [3]

The fund-raising section of the SoS website features a photo of former Florida Secretary of State Katherine Harris—these people can't let anything go—and their mission statement:

> The right wing is always taking extreme measures to bring down President Obama's agenda, even carrying guns to town hall meetings. It's gone too far.[4]

It's like these people did summer internships at the Kremlin learning how to execute a disinformation campaign. The most formidable weapon in the Kremlin's arsenal has always been charges of 'extremism.'[5]

Ritchie was endorsed by ACORN, as was California's Secretary of State Debra Bowen, who is also honored by SoS as "one of the most progressive secretaries of state in the nation." Translation: Don't let this woman near a ballot box.

Obama's boss has gotten too much of his agenda forced through to be willing to retire in 2012.

NOTES

1. Vadum, Matthew. "SOS in Minnesota." *The Spectator*. Nov. 7, 2008. Retrieved from http://spectator.org/archives/2008/11/07/sos-in-minnesota

2. DiscovertheNetworks.com. Retrieved from http://www.discoverthenetworks.org/groupProfile.asp?grpid=7487

3. Patten, David. "ACORN, Soros Linked to Franken Vote Grab." *Newsmax*. Dec. 22, 2008.

4. The Secretary of State Project. Retrieved from http://salsa.wiredforchange.com/o/1356/t/5374/content.jsp?content_KEY=2987

5. Lucas, Edward. *The New Cold War*. Bloomsbury Publishing. 2009.

- 7 -

Our Miss Brooks: Welcome to the Soros Pentagon

One of the many perks of being POTUS, or TOTUS, if you are a stickler for accuracy, is that you don't need to go through the nettlesome process of applying for a security clearance. POTUS gets to decide by fiat what positions should require clearance, and we must accept his appointments as competent patriots, notwithstanding titanic amounts of evidence to the contrary. The president is also at liberty to install incontestably unqualified individuals to sensitive posts.

Absent these prerogatives, there is little likelihood that Rosa Brooks would hold a top position at the Pentagon as adviser to Under Secretary for Defense, Michelle Fluornoy. As a sample of the decorum we can expect from the former *LA Times* op-ed columnist, Brooks described her appointment as her own "personal government bailout." [1]

The former op-ed writer reveals her abysmal lack of understanding of military strategy:

> . . . Brooks depicted the troop surge (in which President Bush sent more than 20,000 additional military personnel to Iraq) as a "feckless plan" that was "too little, too late" and had "no realistic likelihood" of leading to "an enduring solution in Iraq." Subsequent events would prove Brooks wrong; the surge turned the tide of the war dramatically in America's favor. [2]

Anything the daughter of socialist author, Barbara Ehrenreich, lacks in job qualifications, she makes up for via her special kinship with unrepentant Nazi collaborator, George Soros. Brooks served as special counsel to Soros' Open Society Institute. She also has been a consultant for Human Rights Watch and a board member for Amnesty International.[3]

During the Clinton administration, Brooks worked as a senior adviser to berserk transnationalist, Harold Koh, Obama's pick for the top legal position at the State Department.

Miss Brooks used her column at the LA Times chiefly to rant about former President Bush, referring to the administration as a "homegrown" authoritarian government, analogizing the Bush administration to the regimes in North Korea and Iran. She merited her place in the Obama administration by referring to Bush as "our torturer in chief."[4]

A devout Soros toady, Brooks is far more sanguine in her assessment of al-Qaida:

> In 2007 Brooks portrayed al-Qaida as an organization that, prior to 9/11, had been 'little more than an obscure group of extremist thugs, well financed and intermittently lethal, but relatively limited in their global and regional political pull.' 'On 9/11,' she continued, 'they [al-Qaida] got lucky.... Thanks to U.S. policies, al-Qaida has become the vast global threat the [Bush] administration imagined it to be in 2001.' [5]

As is customary with Obama's retinue, Brooks has expressed the *de rigueur* antipathy for Israel, insisting that Israel's recent campaign to stop relentless attacks by Hamas was motivated by political, rather than security, concerns.

George Soros now has a mole in the Pentagon, and not in some grunt post. She is adviser to one of the most powerful people in the organization. Brooks-Soros is already shaping U.S. policy in Afghanistan and crafting our al Qaida strategy. The *Telegraph UK* recently ran a column expressing anxiety about Brooks.[6]

Score one for George Soros. Even the Clinton years weren't this good to him.

nOTES

1. Gardiner, Nile. "Rosa Brooks, The Pentagon's Far Left Advisor." *The Daily Telegraph.* 16, April 2009. Retrieved from **http://blogs.telegraph.co.uk/nile_gardiner/blog/2009/04/16/rosa_brooks_the_pentagons_far_left_adviser.**

2. **DiscovertheNetworks.org.** **http://www.discoverthenetworks.org/individualProfile.asp?indid=2391**

3. Tiz, Joy. *Canada Free Press.* Feb. 18, 2009. **http://canadafreepress.com/index.php/article/8574**

4. *LA Times.* Brooks, Rosa. "A Really Bad Case of Reality." July 20, 2007. Retrieved from **http://articles.latimes.com/2007/jul/20/opinion/oe-brooks20**

5. Klein, Aaron. "Pentagon Official Blames U.S. for al-Qaida Attacks;" *World Net Daily.* April 20, 2009.

6. Gardiner. The Telegraph.

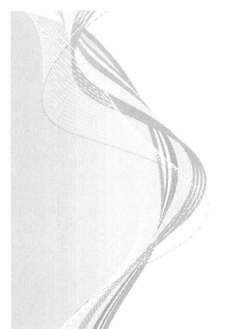

- 8 -

Obama's Boss Demands Show Trials

Attorney General Eric Holder's abominable plot to try self-proclaimed 9/11 mastermind, Khalid Sheik Mohammed (KSM) in a New York criminal court is an affront but not inscrutable. Team O is, as in all other policies, doing the bidding of Obama's boss, unrepentant Nazi collaborator, George Soros; he's been a rabid critic of the war on terror for years.

Soros has always thought we made too much commotion about 9/11, which he insists is just a "single event." He sees 9/11 as no more iniquitous than making prisoners wear underwear on their heads. As an active contributor to the Final Solution (*Obamanutz*), Soros regards the extermination of 3,000 Americans singularly uninspiring:

In fact, Mr. Soros, while conceding that the Sept. 11 attack was a bad thing, wonders why Americans got quite so upset about it. 'How could a single event, even if it involved three thousand civilian casualties, have such a far-reaching effect?' he asks, apparently sincerely. The answer seems to lie 'not so much in the event itself but in the way the United States, under the leadership of President George W. Bush, responded to it.'[1]

Byron York explains the Soros Doctrine for dealing with terrorism:

Mr. Soros is most distressed by the president's war on terrorism. He feels that, in general, the U.S. should deal with the terrorist threat by giving out more foreign aid, enacting more equitable trade laws and being a more constructive, cooperative member of the world community. Mr. Soros argues that the U.S. should have treated the Sept. 11 attacks as a criminal matter, not an act of war. 'Crime requires police work, not military action,' he writes.[2]

Soros certainly puts his money where his mouth is. Among the recipients of his largesse are various terrorist dregs as well as convicted terrorist co-conspirator attorney, Lynne Stewart.[3]

Senator Lindsey Graham asked Eric Holder forthrightly if he could cite a single prior case in which an enemy combatant like KSM had been tried in a criminal court. If Lindsey Graham can make you sputter and writhe, your reasoning must be pretty puerile.

Of course Holder had no answer because there wasn't one. There is no precedent for trying enemy combatants in criminal courts.

Graham's fait accompli came when he asked a befuddled Holder whether he would try Osama bin Laden in a criminal court. That question bared the fatuousness of the entire enterprise.

The whole show trial scheme is yet another placation offering to Soros who craves the opportunity to prosecute the Bush administration:

> A fund-raising letter has revealed one of the leading figures pushing for an investigation of alleged U.S. torture of terror suspects following 9/11: leftist billionaire-financier George Soros.
>
> Officials at the Open Society Institute, which was founded by Soros in 1993 to promote progressive causes around the globe and which bills itself as 'a Soros Foundation Network,' issued an e-mail to supporters announcing the creation of a new organization called the Commission on Accountability."

> On its website, the Commission on Account-
> ability demands an 'independent, non-partisan'
> investigation of 'torture and cruel, inhuman and
> degrading treatment of detainees.' [4]

The only defense Holder can proffer for his bedlamite attitude is the one his boss favors: to change the way the world sees the United States.

Obama supporters still chant that one when pressed to name a single thing their inamorata has done right: "He's changing the way the world sees us!"

Obama has most assuredly changed the way the world sees America. To date, America has not benefited one whit from this new vision.

But that's not the point. All that matters is keeping Obama's boss happy.

NOTES

1. Tiz. Joy. *Obamanutz: A Cult Leader Takes the White House.*

2. York, Byron. *Wall Street Journal.*
   http://www.opinionjournal.com/la/?id=110004486

3. Tiz, Joy. "Obama Boss Supports Terrorism. 18, Nov. 2009.

4. Patten, David. "Billionaire Soros Bankrolling Calls for 'Torture' Probe".
   Newsmax.com. 23, April 2009.

- 9 -

Obama's Boss Scolds Him in Public

Frustrated by the president's inability to follow simple instructions, Obama's boss, unrepentant Nazi collaborator, George Soros has resorted to chiding Obama in public.[1] Soros criticized Obama's incompetence in enacting vital parts of the Soros agenda including government takeover of the banks. From the Wall Street Journal:

> Soros carped that the government should have taken over U.S. banks rather than bailing them out. He also asserted that the American people would have been happier if the federal government had socialized the entire banking system.[2]

Bailing out the banks and allowing them to "earn their way out of the hole" was the wrong solution, according to Obama's overlord.

Imagine how irked Soros must be; first his dreams of death panels were exposed. And as if driven by some Constitutional mandate inscrutable to Democrats, the Supreme Court, in a bolt from the blue, suddenly decided to reaffirm the First Amendment. The dreadful McCain/Feingold bill, another George Soros contrivance, was unconstitutional from the jump.

Obama's boss is keeping a close eye on his lackey to ensure his health care monstrosity gets forced on the American people.

NOTES

1. Tiz, Joy. "Who's Afraid of the Big Bad Soros?" **http://joytiz.com/2010/whos-afraid-of-the-big-bad-soros/**

2. Di Leo, Luca. "Soros Criticizes Obama's Bailouts." *The Wall Street Journal*. March 1, 2010.

- 10 -

But He Can't Fire Soros

> We've tried 19 months of government-as-community organizer. It hasn't worked. Our fresh start needs to begin now.
>
> — John Boehner

House minority leader John Boehner called out the community-organizer-in-chief for his calamitous management of the nation's economy.

> I have had enough—and the American people have had enough—of Washington politicians talking about wanting to create jobs as a ploy to get themselves re-elected while doing everything possible to prevent jobs from being created. [1]

Not that the moribund media would tell you, but Boehner delivered his remarks at a speech before the City Club of Cleveland. Noting the current administration's highly effective War on Jobs, Boehner reflected on Obama's recent visit to Ohio while a few blocks away, Ohioans were standing in line at a job fair, waiting to be told that companies are not hiring.

> They're frozen. Or, as the organizer of the job fair put it, employers are—and I'm quoting now—'scared to death.'

Boehner correctly pointed out that the threat of a lame duck session in which Democrats can ram through more onerous legislation will crush the remaining life out of American businesses.[2] The horrific card check bill is not quite dead yet. The Orwellian-named Employee Free Choice Act would only increase the power of union bosses at the expense of small business.[3]

Boehner also called for the resignations of Tim Geithner and Larry Summers, suggesting that Obama's team lacks actual work experience. Actually, Obama himself did have a real job once. According to CNN's Ed Henry, Obama embezzled from his employer.

> The funny thing was: his high school classmates were telling me that a young Barry Obama used to scoop ice cream at Baskin-Robbins. They said on the side, he used to slip them some free ice cream and frozen yogurt. I sort of have coaxed it out of them because they didn't want

> to acknowledge it at first. And I said, look, 'the
> statute of limitations is past, it's been 30 years
> now.' They laughed and said, 'OK, he gave us
> free ice cream.'[4]

The loss of Geithner would be especially poignant for the president. They go back a long way. Obama's mother, Ann Dunham, worked for Geithner 's father, Peter Geithner, at the Ford Foundation in Indonesia, developing the Foundation's microfinance program.

Obama can certainly do away with Geithner and Summers, but the real problem is Obama's boss, unrepentant Nazi collaborator, George Soros, whose agenda is being forced on an unwilling public.[5] Granted, Obama is light on actual job experience, but even he should realize you can't fire your boss.

NOTES

1. Lopez, Kathryn Jean. "Summers and Geithner Should Go." *National Review*; Aug. 24, 2010.

2. Tiz, Joy. "When Lame Ducks Attack." April 30, 2010.

3. Tiz, Joy. "The Devil Wears Purple." June 29, 2010.

4. Tiz, Joy. "Obama Embezzles from Former Employer." Jan. 1, 2010

5. Tiz, Joy. "Who's Afraid of the Big Bad Soros." Feb. 3, 2010.

-]] -

Soros' Idol: Suppress Disagreement by Force

Addressing the graduates of Hampton University in Virginia, the President of the United States denounced the curse of free flowing information:

> The '24/7 media environment,' he told the students, 'bombards us with all kinds of comments and exposes us to all kinds of arguments, some of which don't always rank all that high on the truth meter.' [1]

Circumventing the courts, the FCC's latest ploy is to reclassify broadband Internet service as a utility, allowing the net to be regulated like telephone service.[2] Free of government intrusion, the Internet has been an engine of conspicuous economic growth and the last citadel for entrepreneurs. Thus, the Obama administration now finds it abhorrent and needs to crush the life out of it with onerous regulations.

> Consider the words of one of the leading advocates of Internet regulation, Robert McChesney, founder of the left-wing group Free Press. McChesney said to *Socialist Project*: 'What we want to have in the U.S. and in every society is an Internet that is not private property, but a public utility.'[3]
>
> He went on to explain: 'At the moment, the battle over network neutrality is not to completely eliminate the telephone and cable companies. We are not at that point yet. But the ultimate goal is to get rid of the media capitalists in the phone and cable companies and to divest them from control.'[4]

We're already feeling the repercussions of Obama's latest socialist contrivance: heavy losses in cable and telecommunication stocks the day after FCC chairman, Julius Genachowski, announced he would start proceedings to classify broadband companies as "telecommunication services." [5]

By midday in New York, shares in Time Warner Cable and Cablevision were down more than 6 percent, while Comcast had fallen almost 5 percent. Cable operators account for most U.S. Internet connections, but telecoms groups also fell, with AT&T off 1.1 percent and Verizon Communications down 0.3 percent.

The economic havoc that will be wrought by a government take-over of the Internet is but one lagniappe for the administration.

The job of the press is supposed to be to follow politicians around and write down what they say and do. Our Founding Fathers thought the right of the press to perform that specific job was important enough to address it in the very first amendment to our Constitution. Under English common law, wrongful statements against government officials could result in jail or fines. Our Founders understood the essential service provided by a free press in protecting a fledgling democracy. If the system was working as it should, politicians and reporters would be natural enemies.

The American mainstream media was hijacked by the Left some time ago, but not until Barack Obama came along did the press become a true ministry of propaganda. No politician has exploited the media to the degree that Obama has.

Only Fox News and the alternative media have failed to obey. The new Democrat talking point is that we Americans need to be defended against "unfiltered information."

> In this administration, freedom of speech, press or information is a distraction and a threat. That's why they sought to impose the doctrine of 'net neutrality' on the Internet. In the name of opening up broadband to all, it's designed to suppress the voices of those who have competed in the marketplace of ideas and won. [6]

If you scrape all the way down to the barrel's bottom, you will find that Obama's puppet master, George Soros, is an advocate for controlling public opinion — by force, if necessary.

In addition to being God and the Pope's boss, George Soros likes to think of himself as a great philosopher.[7] Indeed, his interest in philosophy far outweighs his fascination with business. Something of an investing savant, Soros considers his wealth to be the tool by which he can reshape the world to his liking. His biggest obstacle is the United States.

Lacking in any genuine creativity of his own, Soros eventually glommed onto the work of Karl Popper who concocted the theory of the *Open Society*. Against the backdrop of Hitler's invasion of Austria, Popper opined that totalitarianism creates "closed societies."

Popper argued that humans have only two possible destinies. One is to live in a closed society in which everyone is forced to believe the same thing. The other would be an open society free of nationalisms and tribal wars. Open society, freedom — sounds harmless enough, right?

Soros' and his idol have their own spin on what tolerance is all about:

If we extend unlimited tolerance even to those who are intolerant, if we are not prepared to defend a tolerant society against the onslaught of the intolerant, then the tolerant will be destroyed, and tolerance with them. In this formulation, I do not imply, for instance, that we should always suppress the utterance of intolerant philosophies; as long as we can counter them by rational argument and keep them in check by public opinion, suppression would certainly be most unwise. But we should claim the right to suppress them if necessary even by force; for it may easily turn out that they are not prepared to meet us on the level of rational argument, but begin by denouncing all argument; they may forbid their followers to listen to rational argument, because it is deceptive , and teach them to answer arguments by the use of their fists or pistols. We should therefore claim, in the name of tolerance, the right not to tolerate the intolerant.[8]

-The Open Society and Its Enemies:
The Spell of Plato, by Karl Raimund Popper.

To paraphrase: Open government, to Soros' idol, means people can freely express their views as long as they agree with us. If they don't agree with us, and we can't convince them that they should agree with us, it's perfectly fine to suppress them by force. We can do this, of course, because this is for their own good — people who aren't smart enough to agree with us shouldn't be allowed to participate in their government.

NOTES

1. Investors.com. "The President's Trick or Tweet." May 5, 2010. Retrieved from **http://www.investors.com/NewsAndAnalysis/Article. aspx?id=532832**

2. Kerpin, Phil. *Fox News*. "The FCC Goes for Nuclear Option." May 6, 2010.

3. *The Bullet*, "An Interview with Robert McChesney." E-Bulletin No. 246. August 9, 2009

4. Ibid

5. "FCC Backs Google/Soros 'Net Neutrality.' *Sweetness & Light*. Retrieved from **http://sweetness-light.com/archive/fcc-backs-googlesoros-net-neutrality**

6. *Investors.com*. "The President's Trick or Tweet." 10, May 2010. Retrieved from **http://www.investors.com/NewsAndAnalysis/Article. aspx?id=532832**

7. Tiz, Joy. "Soros: It's Not Easy Being God." April 7, 2010.

8. Valinska, Ellie. "Obama's Open Government, Soros's Open Society and Popper's Crazy Ideas." *Big Bureaucracy*. Feb. 2, 2010.

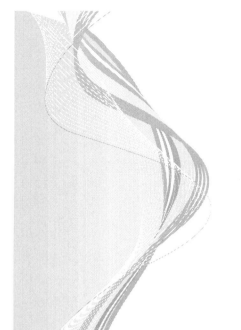

- 12 -

Soros Hearts Cap and Tax

Placing himself on the same side of the Cap and Trade debate as Osama bin Laden, Puppet Master in Chief, George Soros, is supporting the ruinous legislation.[1]

Donny Ferguson at Western Tradition Partnership reports:

> Blogger *FITSNews.com* reveals left-wing environmentalist groups are bankrolling ads in South Carolina backing Graham's radical green agenda, including one ad buy of $10,000 alone. The ads are purchased by GMMB, a Washington, D.C. media broker that advises President Barack Obama.

'Republicans for Environmental Protection,' which is connected to a George Soros donor fund provides 'fiscal sponsorship for progressive groups.'[2]

Soros is a big fan of environmental regulation. Last year he pledged to invest a billion dollars in "clean energy technology." [3]

When Soros throws around that kind of money, rest assured that his aims are entirely nefarious. He suddenly developed an interest in a little mining town in Romania just as a Canadian company proposed to mine their gold, generating income for the villagers.

The impoverished village of Rosia Montana, Romania, is blessed with gold. The village's last best hope to escape crushing poverty was blocked by environmental groups, NGO's and — George Soros.

The left-wing dominated media has falsely reported that the village would prefer to eschew indoor plumbing to defend itself from the Canadian mining company proposing to mine the gold.

The great philanthropist, coincidentally enough, opened the Soros Foundation Romania in Rosia Montana. His grand opening was booed by the locals who are in dire need of the revenue from the mine. Historically, the village derives its only income from mining.

Tragically, Soros won, aided and abetted by a shameless mainstream media. The Rosia mine chicanery is an excellent case study

in Sorosian deception. He affects the most altruistic of motives —
in this case, the liberation of a little Romanian village from the
evil corporatists. His sycophants in the media provide the cover
and he walks away with the prize.

NOTES

1. Tiz, Joy. "Bin Laden Endorses Can-N-Tax." 29, Jan. 2010

2. Ferguson, Donny. "WTP warns Graham: Drop national energy tax, radical green support." *Western Tradition Partnership*. April 26, 2010. Retrieved from **http://www.westerntradition.org/?p=764**

3. Manhire, Tony. "George Soros Pledges $1bn to Search for Clean Energy." *The Guardian*. Oct. 12, 2009.

- 13 -

Regulation for You, But Not for Soros

Puppet Master and unrepentant Nazi collaborator, George Soros is poised for a big win with the proposed financial "reform" feculence being phonied up by Chris "Countrywide" Dodd and the rest of the corruptocrats.

Author and businessman Zubi Diamond is critical of the Managed Funds Association (MFA), a lobby group championing the protection of hedge funds, including Soros' own Quantum Fund, from scrutiny.

> The hedge fund short sellers, who are members of the Managed Funds Association, are running our government today. They are the ones who authored the Dodd bill. The Dodd bill is punishing the victims of the hedge fund short sellers. The Dodd bill is punishing the good Wall Street. [1]

The Puppet Master, naturally, is the leading member of the MFA, according to Diamond, as well as its busiest and most influential member.

The repeal of the uptick rule and other safeguards enable unregulated hedge funds to wreak market mayhem:

Diamond says that the repeal of the safeguard regulations, such as the uptick rule, circuit breakers and trading curbs, and the introduction of the short ETFs (Exchange Traded Funds), which began under Christopher Cox at the Securities and Exchange Commission, has given the members of the MFA tremendous power and influence. He says these individuals include George Soros, John Paulson, Jim Chanos, James Simon, and other hedge fund short sellers, including those who operate Quant Funds and engage in computerized trading. [2]

The uptick rule essentially operated as a circuit breaker to prevent complete catastrophe driven by market exploitation. The removal of the uptick rules allows hedge fund short sellers to manipulate stock prices by triggering panic selling.

> Many people do not realize that the hedge funds are responsible for 75-90 percent of all trading activities on Wall Street. They are responsible for the extreme market volatility. They are responsible for everything that is bad on Wall Street. [3]

Soros wants the Obama administration to have absolute domination over the stocks in your 401K while allowing cyclopean hedge funds to operate entirely unregulated, unregistered and in stealth.

> An example of the bad Wall Street would be someone like George Soros. These people are the financial hedge fund short-selling operators who make money by betting on company collapse, economic calamities and catastrophes.
>
> Soros and his collaborators have an anti-capitalism agenda, an anti-industrialized nation agenda, and a far-left liberal, Marxist radical agenda. Most hedge fund short sellers are not capitalist. They are anti-capitalist and they are not investors. They are anti-investors. They succeed when companies (or countries) fail.

> The bad Wall Street, in the form of the hedge fund short sellers, engineered the economic collapse, looted every portfolio that had exposure to the stock market, and blamed George Bush and the Republicans, enabling Barack Obama and his backers, including Soros, to take power. [4]

Diamond recommends putting our regulatory system back to what it was in 2006—before Chris Cox became SEC chairman. In other words, reverse the changes lobbied for by the MFA:

> The only financial reform needed today is to regulate and monitor the hedge funds and the hedge fund short sellers, some of which are registered off-shore to avoid scrutiny. These global operators, with investors who remain mostly anonymous, must be compelled to register with the Securities and Exchange Commission (SEC), publicly disclose their positions in the markets, and maintain accounting and trading records for a period of 10 years so their activities can be monitored and scrutinized. Just like mutual funds, they must be prohibited from engaging in day trading activities. [5]

Putting hedge funds under scrutiny is not an anti-free market move. The Soros-led Obama administration is fiercely anti-capitalist. Such is the hypocrisy of the left—loot the system while lecturing the rest of us about greed.

The hedge fund short sellers looted $11 trillion from the U.S. economy. They walk away with all our invested capital and they walk away with the intrinsic profit from devalued home mortgages (our homes) through short selling. Yet, no one goes to jail. Why? Answer: They are too chummy with the Obama administration. The looters have been given a seat at the table in the White House. They are being protected by our government.[6]

Diamond warns:

As an immigrant who came to America to achieve success, I understand the stakes, perhaps more than most. This is a fight to save America, to save capitalism and protect us from the disaster of socialism.

I know that the liberals, who say they want to help the poor, think that the solution is socialism. But socialism never helps the poor; it only traps them indefinitely in poverty. You will never have a rags-to-riches story in a socialist economy. Liberation from poverty is only possible through capitalism. [7]

NOTES

1. Diamond, Zubi. The Dodd 'Financial Reform Bill Lets Soros Off the Hook. *GOPUSA.* April 5, 2010.

2. Kincaid, Cliff. "Manipulation, Not Error, Behind Market Plunge." *Accuracy in Media.* May 7, 2010.

2. Phillips, Matt. "New Short Selling Rules... Explained." *The Wall Street Journal.* Feb. 24, 2010

3. Diamond, Zubi. "The Dodd 'Financial Reform Bill Lets Soros Off the Hook." *GOPUSA.* April 5, 2010.

4. Ibid.

5. Ibid.

6. Ibid

7. Ibid

- 14 -

Soros Facing Defeat In Missouri

The Puppet Master, unrepentant Nazi collaborator, George Soros is trying to thwart the democratic process yet again. In Missouri, voters may have the opportunity to put an end to crony justice:.

Under an initiative headed for the ballot in November, the state's so-called merit selection method would be discarded and replaced by direct judicial elections, an outcome that would be an embarrassment to many who have pushed the Missouri plan as a model for other states. Used in some form by more than 30 states, the Missouri plan requires that vacancies be filled through an ostensibly nonpartisan judicial nominating commission. The commission selects a

> slate of potential judges from which the governor chooses a nominee. [1]

The effect of the current system has been to hand a third of the state government over to one profession with minimal accountability. The notion of we the people having input into the selection of judges is deeply offensive to Soros:

> The system has powerful defenders, however, including groups connected to the George Soros-funded Justice at Stake. And in Missouri, the response to the ballot measure has been fast and furious. Missouri Bar President H.A. Walther railed that the proposal would 'put a price tag on each of the seven seats on our state supreme court.'
>
> Former Missouri Supreme Court Judge and trial lawyer Chip Robertson and his Soros-affiliated 'Missourians for Fair and Impartial Courts' took to hassling the ballot initiative's signature gatherers, using 'blockers' to discourage voters from signing petitions. But the initiative has so far survived all court challenges. [2]

Let's hope the wise voters of the Show Me state take their power back and away from George Soros.

NOTES

1. "Voters vs. George Soros." *The Wall Street Journal.* June 2, 2010.
   http://online.wsj.com/article/SB100014240527487043707045752284619 14892980.html

2. Ibid.

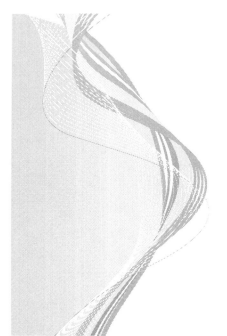

- 15 -

Obama's Boss Sees Silver Lining in BP Spill

Reuters is reporting that Brazil stands to benefit from the BP oil spill catastrophe as the U.S. moratorium makes more rigs available for other countries.

> Even as an ecological catastrophe makes the future of U.S. offshore drilling less certain, Brazil is plowing ahead with a $220 billion five-year plan to tap oil fields even deeper than BP's (BP.L) ill-fated Gulf well, which is still leaking crude.[1]

It's estimated that thirty five rigs are now sitting idle in the Gulf of Mexico. Brazil is already getting inquiries from companies wanting to move their rigs there. Brazil's state oil company, Petrobras already produces about a fourth of the world's deep water oil.

> Analysts say oil companies operating in the Gulf of Mexico—most notably BP and Chevron (CVX.N)—may have to decide between paying standby fees while the rigs are idle, moving them to other projects, or canceling the contracts.
>
> The U.S. moratorium may last longer than six months because of U.S. sentiment against off-shore drilling and plans for an overhaul of safety standards.

The shortage of rigs could help Brazil become a major oil exporter.

What an amazing stroke of good fortune for Obama's boss, unrepentant Nazi collaborator, George Soros!

Soros is also invested in offshore oil drilling in Brazil, assisted by the American taxpayers.

Newsmax:

> The Wall Street Journal reports: 'The United States, through the U.S. Export-Import Bank, has issued a 'preliminary commitment' of $2 billion and more if needed' to Petroleo Brasileiro SA, a Brazilian government-owned oil exploration and development corporation known as 'Petrobras.' [2]

Soros Fund Management, LLC holds a stake in Petrobras of approximately $900 million as of December 31, 2009.

> George Soros' principal investments are in oil; one in particular is Petrobras, the Brazilian-owned company. This happens to be the largest investment in the Soros portfolio at the present time.
>
> Now that word is out that the facilities of the U.S. Export-Import Bank SA is offering guarantees for loans to Brazil's state-owned oil company Petrobras, U.S. citizens are beginning to complain.

Soros also owns quite a lot of real estate in Brazil. Soros' Adeco-agro, which invests in renewable energy, owns or leases about 840,000 acres of farmland in Argentina, Brazil and Uruguay growing coffee, soybeans and other commodities. Royal Dutch Shell Plc and Bunge Ltd. Are also expanding into ethanol in Brazil.

When you get to boss the president around, you never have to let a good crisis go to waste.

NOTES

1. *Reuters.* "Brazil Sees Silver Lining in BP Spill: More Rigs." 11 June 2010. http://www.reuters.com/article/idUSN1115006620100611

2. Hostetter, Ralph. "U.S. Gov't., Soros Fund Offshore Drilling in Brazil." *Newsmax.* 11 February 2010. http://www.newsmax.com/hostetter/hostetter-Soros-Obama-economy/2010/02/11/id/349645

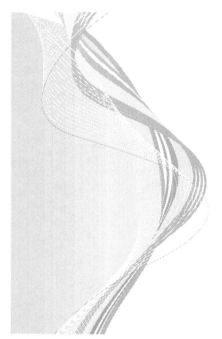

- 16 -

Guess Who Else Hearts Brazil?

illary Clinton has lauded the Brazilian economy as "growing like crazy" as a result of high taxation. The Secretary of State is suddenly bleating about the brutal unfairness inherent in not forcing Americans to fork over even more of their income to the all mighty government. Clinton:

> Brazil has the highest tax-to-GDP rate in the Western Hemisphere and guess what—they're growing like crazy. [1]

The *American Thinker* reminds us that Clintonian "facts" are chimerical things:

> But, as with any 'fact' a Clinton or an Obama apparatchik cites, you need to look it up for yourself. Which I did. Brazil's GDP grew 2.0% in the last quarter. The average rates for 2007, 2008 and 2009 were 1.61%, 0.39% and 0.96%, respectively.[80]
>
> For those who may be wondering, our own GDP growth in the last quarter was 3.00%. But I digress. The point is: Either (1) Hillary didn't know Brazil's actual growth rate; (2) she did know, but lied about it or (3) she knew and considers 3.00% GDP growth 'growing like crazy.' Pick any one, two, or—this *is* the Obama administration, after all—all three.[2]

Coincidentally, the Puppet Master himself—unrepentant Nazi collaborator, George Soros, has gone sweet on Brazil too:

> Billionaire George Soros's Adecoagro venture, which invests in agriculture and renewable energy in Latin America, is considering an initial public offering to help fund projects in Brazil that include a $700 million sugar mill.

> Soros' Adecoagro owns or leases about 840,000 acres of farmland in Argentina, Brazil and Uruguay, growing coffee, soybeans and other commodities. Royal Dutch Shell Plc and Bunge Ltd. are also expanding into ethanol in Brazil.
>
> Adecoagro, founded in 2002 by investors including Soros to buy Argentine farmland after the peso crashed, plans to more than double sugar-cane crushing in Brazil to 11 million metric tons by 2016, from 4.8 million now, and also build a 6 million-ton cane processor in Mato Grosso do Sul state this year. It also may buy a Brazilian sugar mill, Vieira said, in Sao Paulo.[3]

Always one to hedge his bets, Soros is also invested in offshore oil drilling in Brazil, assisted by the American taxpayers. *Newsmax*:

> The Wall Street Journal reports: 'The United States, through the U.S. Export-Import Bank, has issued a 'preliminary commitment' of $2 billion and more if needed' to Petroleo Brasileiro SA, a Brazilian government-owned oil exploration and development corporation known as 'Petrobras.'

Soros Fund Management, LLC holds a stake in Petrobras of approximately $900 million as of December 31, 2009.

George Soros' principal investments are in oil; one in particular is Petrobras, the Brazilian-owned company. This happens to be the largest investment in the Soros portfolio at the present time. Now that word is out that the facilities of the U.S. Export-Import Bank SA is offering guarantees for loans to Brazil's state-owned oil company Petrobras, U.S. citizens are beginning to complain.[4]

How darned sporting of Hillary to take time out from her busy schedule to talk up her boss's Brazilian investments.

NOTES

1. Schwimmer, Gene. "Hillary: Brazil Growing Like Crazy." *American Thinker.* May 28, 2010.

2. Ibid.

3. Kassai, Lucia. "Soros-Backed Venture Weighs IPO to Fund Brazil Mill. *Bloomberg Businessweek.* Feb. 2, 2010

4. Hostetter, Ralph. "U.S. Gov't, Soros Funds Offshore Drilling in Brazil." *NewsMax.* Feb. 11, 2010

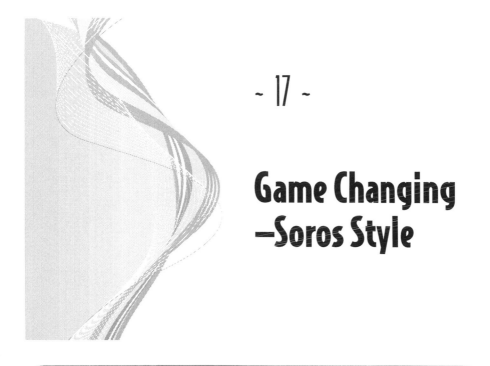

- 17 -

Game Changing –Soros Style

> *When Binder showed them video of Obama, they were struck by his sincerity, his genuineness, his not-the-same-old-politician-ness.*
>
> — Game Change

I t must be really swell to be a "journalist"; you can name your book after one of the year's most tired catch phrases and be free from the hardship of having to identify the sources of your "facts. *Game Change*, by John Heilemann and Mark Halperin purports to present the parallel stories inside the campaigns during the 2008 election. The authors declined to share their sources for all of this detailed insider information.

Apparently, being a journalist also confers psychic powers — Heilemann and Halperin often were able to read minds:

"She [Hillary] was like Cassandra, convinced she could see the future, filled with angst that no one believed her." (Pg. 231).

Mark Halperin is senior political analyst for *Time*. What you've not heard in the media is that Mark Halperin is also the red diaper brat son of Morton Halperin, currently senior advisor to the Open Society Institute (OSI).

The senior Halperin is an outspoken advocate of American nuclear disarmament [1]

Incredibly, Halperin wrote in 1971 that the Soviet Union never considered use of military force against Western Europe, insisting that the Soviet posture has been and continued to be a defensive one, protecting itself against *us*.

From 1961 to 1966 he taught at Harvard University's Center for International Affairs. During this period, he advocated U.S. nuclear disarmament even if the Soviet Union did not likewise disarm. In any mutual arms reduction treaty with the Soviets, wrote Halperin in his 1961 treatise A Proposal for a Ban on the Use of Nuclear Weapons, "inspection was not absolutely necessary . . . The United States might, in fact . . . interested in them. [2]

Morton Halperin has a long history of anti-Americanism:

'Morton Halperin is dangerous,' said Senator Strom Thurmond of this man, nominated to shape national security policy and to again have access to America's most highly classified military secrets. After the U.S. Senate refused to confirm Halperin, President Clinton appointed the controversial left-wing activist to several positions that required no Senate confirmation: Special Assistant to the President, Senior Director for Democracy at the National Security Council and consultant to the Secretary of Defense and to the Under Secretary of Defense for Policy.

'In 1998, Halperin became director of policy planning for the U.S. State Department. During his tenure 15 State Department laptop computers containing highly classified intelligence information disappeared, one of them checked out to Halperin's office. Others were punished for this serious security breach, but Halperin was not.' [3]

Thus, Morton is a perfect fit for OSI, working closely with Obama's boss, unrepentant Nazi collaborator, George Soros.

As another acorn that didn't fall far from the tree, young Mark has racked up a long rap sheet of journalistic misdeeds.

Having helped Clinton win, Mark Halperin then covered the President-elect's transition to power and 'was assigned to White House coverage for the first two years of the Clinton administration.'

'Apparently it bothered neither ABC nor Halperin that this network's White House reporter was the son of high-level Clinton appointee and controversial presidential advisor Morton Halperin. In 1997, the same year Mark Halperin was promoted to Political Director of ABC News, his brother David began a four-year stint as speechwriter to President Clinton.'

Halperin's 2004 Bush-criticizing memo was controversial not only in its content but also in its timing. It was delivered to ABC News personnel including 'Good Morning America' co-host Charlie Gibson only hours before Gibson was to select audience questions for – and to moderate between – the participants of the second Presidential Debate: President Bush and Senator Kerry. It is hard not to see this as Halperin trying to have an anti-Bush influence on how Gibson framed the debate.' 4

If you've been wondering whether this cliché ridden screed is worth your time, allow me to summarize: everyone involved in the 2008 campaign who was not part of Team O is crazy, incompetent, or both. Barack Obama courageously saved the world from economic bedlam in September of 2008 during the celebrated meeting with Bush, McCain , Paulson, et al. No details are provided as to exactly how Obama rescued the free world — presumably, his mere presence was sufficient.

There is the occasional nugget of truth: "Financial economics was hardly an area of expertise for Obama . . . " (Pg. 378). No indication as to his mastery of non-financial economics. In any case, Obama wisely called a bunch of really smart guys to get himself au courant.

So smitten are Heilemann and Halperin, that the book is remarkably free of criticism of Obama other than a few altogether believable passages about his incessant bellyaching about how "hard" it is to run for leader of the free world.

As with most things Obama, the trail eventually leads back to his boss, George Soros.

NOTES

1. *Open Society Foundations.*
   http://www.soros.org/initiatives/washington/about/bios/halperin

2. *Discover the Networks.org* http://www.discoverthenetworks.org/
   individualProfile.asp?indid=1682

3. Lowell, Ponte. "The ABC's of Media Bias." *Frontpagemag.com.* 14
   October 2004. http://archive.frontpagemag.com/readArticle.
   aspx?ARTID=10987

4. Ibid.

About the Author

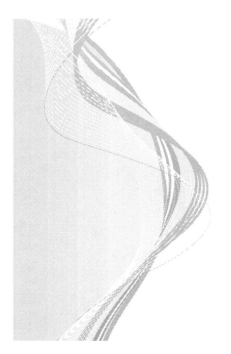

Joy was born in Chicago, long enough ago to remember when many democrats were actually normal people who were just wrong about everything. Joy holds a M.Sc. in psychology and a JD in law. Joy was a columnist at America's Voices and has written on politics and current events. Her new book, *Obamanutz: A Cult Leader Takes the White House* exposes the machinery that enabled Barack Obama to grab the highest office in the land.

Joy is available to speak at Tea Party and other events nationwide.

Joy is also the owner of three magnificent and staunchly conservative German Shepherds, a Quarter Horse mare lacking in work ethic and Zirc the Wonder Colt.

Joy Tiz, MS, JD
www.joytiz.com

Made in the USA
Lexington, KY
26 July 2011